IN MY BANANAS

lots of funny poems

Neal Zetter

Illustrated by Chris White

Published by TROIKA BOOKS

This edition published 2017
Troika Books
Well House, Green Lane, Ardleigh CO7 7PD, UK

www.troikabooks.com

A CIP catalogue record for this book
is available from the British Library

ISBN 978-1-909991-58-3

1 2 3 4 5 6 7 8 9 10

Printed in Poland

Some Words from the Poet...

There was an old lady from Hull
And she bumped into a bull
The bull said "Ow!"
Crashed into a cow
Then the cow smashed into the wall

Well I was the tender age of six when I wrote that poem - my very first ever. Quite a few years on I am pleased to say that it was the earliest step on my road to becoming a professional poet during which time I have run countless poetry writing workshops, performed in hundreds of venues and written over 800 separate pieces of verse. This book showcases a collection of what people tell me are some of my best efforts to date. I hope you enjoy them immensely, I hope you laugh out loud and, most of all, I hope you are inspired to write your own poetry.

Neal Zetter
www.cccpworkshops.co.uk

CONTENTS

I'm a Bee

I'm a bee
I'm a bee
Buzzing round your head
Hear my sound all around
Like a very long zed
I'm not an A or a C
Or a D or an E
'Cause I'm a bee
I'm a bee
I'm a bee, bee, bee

I'm a bee
I'm a bee
Coloured yellow and black
I've got wings and a sting
So I might attack
My queen is the one
Who's a mum to me
I'm a bee
I'm a bee
I'm a bee, bee, bee

I'm a bee
I'm a bee
So loving that honey
Sit for hours on the flowers
In the summer when it's sunny
In my hive I survive
High up in a tree
I'm a bee
I'm a bee
I'm a bee, bee, bee

I'm a bee
I'm a bee
Buzzing round your head
Hear my sound all around
Like a very long zed
I'm not an A or a C
Or a D or an E
I'm a bee
I'm a bee
I'm a bee, bee, bee

I'm a bee
I'm a bee
I'm a bee, bee, bee

I'm a bee
I'm a bee
I'm a bee, bee...
Bee

Ba nana nana nana nana nana nana nana nana nana nana nana nana nana

What's the longest fruit you've seen?
Found in milkshake, yoghurt and ice cream
When they're on my plate I lick it clean
A tremendous taste
Too good to waste
Ba nana nana nana nana nana nana nana nana nana nana
nana nana

You'll slip upon their slimy skin
So put the peel into the bin
What word doesn't stop after it begins?
Simply unending
I'm always bending my
Ba nana nana nana nana nana nana nana nana nana nana
nana nana

You can mash them
You can squash them
You can squish them
You can gulp them
You can fry them
You can spread them
You can pound them
You can pulp them
When I ask what food you've had today
I'm hoping that you're going to say
Ba nana nana nana nana nana nana nana nana nana nana nana
nana nana

Monkeys eat them at the zoo
They're yellow and black not orange and blue
Ideal in soup or in a stew
They're versatile
Shaped like a smile
Ba nana nana nana nana nana nana nana nana nana nana nana
nana nana

Buy them by the kilo, pound or bunch
Stick them in your sandwich box for lunch
They're the ideal snack when it comes to the crunch
Travelling all the way from Jamaica
What fruit's got a name that's a record breaker?
Ba nana nana nana nana nana nana nana nana nana nana nana
nana nana

Before you get some from the store
Shout out this poem's title once more
Ba nana nana nana nana nana nana nana nana nana nana nana
nana nana

Don't annoy that Monster

Don't annoy that monster
Don't tickle his big belly
Don't change the channel
When he's watching monster telly

Don't give his tail a tug
Don't steal his pink pyjamas
Don't make him angry
'Cause he's safer when he's calmer

Don't sit on his baseball cap
Don't wake him up at four
Don't bother him during bath times
Don't remind him that he snores

Don't re-tune his radio
Don't drill holes in his pants
Don't fill his welly boots
With thousands of red ants

Don't eat his chocolate cookies
Don't slurp his strawberry shake
Don't poke your head into his mouth
FOR GOODNESS SAKE!

Don't say to him "You're ugly mate"
Don't scribble on his skin
If you're playing him at football
Then it's best to let him win

Don't jab him with a cricket bat
Don't cover him in jam
Don't drop a melon on his foot
Don't Sellotape his hands

Don't snigger at his haircut
Don't smash into his car
'Cause if you do I'm telling you
He might go
RAAAAAAAAAAAAAAAAAAAAAAAAAAAAAAAAAAAAAH!

The Naughty Chair

I sat upon the Naughty Chair
Because my teacher sent me there
I screamed my head off, pulled my hair
I grizzled like a grizzly bear
Began to curse, began to swear
"This isn't right, this isn't fair!"
The other children laughed and stared
At me upon the Naughty Chair

I sat upon the naughty seat
Began to bawl, began to bleat
 "You're wrong Miss cos I'm innocent
"I never, ever, ever meant
"To stick my thumb up Sophie's nose
"And then to wipe it down her clothes"
I waved my arms, I stamped my feet
When I sat on the naughty seat

I sat upon the naughty stool
I felt embarrassed, looked a fool
For putting salt in teachers' tea
For shouting 'BLAAAAH' in assembly
For sticking chewing gum on doors
For throwing stink bombs on the floor
For burping in the dinner hall
They sat me on the naughty stool

Yes, I sat in that naughty place
Sir yelled "Wipe *that* smile off your face
"You broke the rules, you take the blame
"Now 'Naughty Neal' is your new name
"Sit silent at the back alone
"More messing 'round you'll be sent home"
So be warned, behave if not BEWARE!
Or you'll end up on that Naughty Chair

I'm going out with the invisible Woman

I'm going out with the invisible woman
I'm meeting her for a date
I'm going out with the invisible woman
She said she'd meet me at eight
But she's making me wait
She's one hour late
Though I couldn't find her
If I was standing behind her

I'm going out with the invisible woman
Though what she looks like I don't know
I'm going out with the invisible woman
I could so easily tread on her toe
Or leave without her when we go
To the cinema or to a show
It is quite apparent
My girlfriend's transparent

I'm going out with the invisible woman
I walked right through her last night
I'm going out with the invisible woman
I can't see her though it's broad daylight
Like a polar bear on a background of white
She's out of my sight
The torture I've been through
'Cause my girlfriend's see-through

I'm going out with the invisible woman
Though we've never met face-to-face
I'm going out with the invisible woman
She could be standing in this very place
Though all you see is empty space
Don't say I'm a nutcase!
My girlfriend's invisible - it's true
She just vanishes into the blue

I'm going out with the invisible woman
I'm still waiting here on my own
I'm going out with the invisible woman
Looks like one more evening alone
She's got no skin and bones
But she still could have phoned
I guess I'm not in her future plans
Perhaps she's run off - with the invisible man

AHHHH...CHOOOO!

There's a cold a-coming
So your head is numbing
And your nose is running
AHHHH...CHOOOO!

'Cause before you know it
There's a small storm growing
Yucky stuff is flowing
AHHHH...CHOOOO!

It's a germ-filled potion
It's a huge explosion
Made in one sharp motion
AHHHH...CHOOOO!

Grab a hankie
Grab a tissue
Grab some kitchen roll
From your pocket
Stop that rocket
Shooting like a wonder goal
Zooming out your nostril holes
AHHHHHHHHHHHHHHHHHHHHH...
CHOOOOOOOOOOOOOOOOOOOOO!

When your nasal passage
Unloads all its baggage
Greener than a cabbage
AHHHH...CHOOOO!

No-one's gonna love ya
'Cause here comes another
Careful – mind your brother!
AHHHH...CHOOOO!

Both your eyes are crying
You feel like you're dying
All that virus flying
AHHHH...CHOOOO!

You try so hard to stem your sneezes but there's nothing you can do
They just pop out of the blue
AHHHH...CHOOOO!

They're so loud they can be heard as far away as Timbuktu
Here's the next one in the queue
AHHHH...CHOOOO!

AHHHH...CHOOOO!
AHHHH...CHOOOO!
AHHHH...CHOOOO!
AHHHH...CHOOOO!
AHHHH...CHOOOO!
AHHHH...CHOOOO!
AHHHHHHHHHHHHHHHHHHHHH...
CHOOOOOOOOOOOOOOOOOOOOO!

Sorry!

I'm sorry that I spilt my drink
I'm sorry that I scratched your car
Stained the carpet with black ink
And flicked popcorn in the cinema

I'm sorry I ate all your cakes
The ones that you were saving
I'm sorry I kept our street awake
All last night misbehaving

I'm sorry I failed my maths exam
And that my bedroom's a disgusting mess
I'm sorry I put ants in the apricot jam
And I'm sorry I'm so slow in the morning getting dressed...

I'm sorry that I kicked the cat
And broke the TV remote control
I'm sorry that I smashed your window
When I scored that fantastic goal

I'm sorry I was rude to you
I'm sorry that I swore
I'm sorry I stuck glue to you
And shouted `NO!' to the household chores

I'm sorry that I slapped my sister
So hard upon her leg
I'm sorry that I didn't miss her
When I threw that rotten egg

I'm sorry I was late for school
I'm sorry I lost your house keys
I'm sorry I break all your rules
Like I don't always say `thanks' and `please'

I'm sorry that I told you lies
Left your newspaper out in the rain
And I'm sorry that when I apologise
I then do the same thing again

I'm sorry that I make you sad
I'm sorry that I make you mad
I'm really sorry Mum and Dad
When I'm not good
When I am bad
I'm sorry, sorry, sorry!

I wish I was a Sumo Wrestler

I wish I was a sumo wrestler
I'd never see my feet
My bottom would be big enough to occupy three seats

I wish I was a sumo wrestler
My clothes would never fit me
I'd squash and sit on anyone who punched or kicked or hit me

I wish I was a sumo wrestler
I'd wrestle for a living
I'd eat your whole fridge for my tea plus forty-three roast chickens

I wish I was a sumo wrestler
They'd say "Look at the size of his belly!"
I'd wobble walking down the street just like a giant jelly

I wish I was a sumo wrestler
Heavier than twenty trucks
If you let me in your front door I would probably get stuck

I wish I was a sumo wrestler
A hero from Japan
A bouncy, bouncy, bouncy, bouncy million ouncy man

I wish I was a sumo wrestler
My weight would bust your bed
And I'd cause a massive tidal wave if I swam in the Med

I wish I was a sumo wrestler
As humungous as can be
I'd not fit upon the screen of your portable TV

I wish I was a sumo wrestler
A martial arts gold medal winner
And if YOU sniggered at my stomach's size...
I'D MASH YOU UP FOR DINNER!

The Ultimate Superhero

I'm the Ultimate Superhero
No job's too big or too small
When danger threatens our country
Or if your cat's stuck up a tree
It's me you'll want to call
I'm the Ultimate Superhero

If you're a bad guy then I'm your supreme test
My legs and arms are wider than your expanded chest
You'll recognise me by the golden U.S.H on my vest
And like my fellow superheroes I've a cape to help me fly
If you shot, bashed, squashed or smashed me I'll never die
Though I don't suggest you try
I've even made a Dalek break down and cry
I'm the Ultimate Superhero

I'm indestructible
Undefeatable
Incorruptible
Totally unbeatable
Ultra-intelligent
Flabbergastingly fast
You'll not see me wear an Elastoplast
Or a plaster cast
I'll stop muggers who mug
Robbers who rob
Kidnappers who kidnap
Fighting crime is my job
I'm the Ultimate Superhero

Superman's a gentle pussycat next to me
Batman's a beginner, a novice, a trainee
While Spider-Man's not even in the reckoning
I'll spearhead the attack when danger's beckoning
I pack the most powerful of powerful punches
I start work at six and never stop for tea or lunches
Do you know who the pick of the superhero bunch is?
Me - I'm the Ultimate Superhero

I've got a secret identity like all superheroes do
Who am I? Well, it's a secret - so I'm not telling you
But rest assured I'll be there when I am needed
When the laws of the nation are no longer heeded
I'll be the first in the queue
To protect you
Beating super villains is what I do
So you can sleep safely in your beds at night
You've no need to live in fear, no
Leave it to me
To keep you free
I'm the Ultimate Superhero

Friday is Chip Day

Friday is Chip Day
A love to lick your lips day
What do all our teachers say?
Friday is Chip Day

Friday is a top day
The chips just never stop day
Not pork pie or lamb chop day
Friday is Chip Day

Friday is a great day
No need to watch your weight day
A run to the school gate day
Friday is Chip Day

Friday is the best day
A zip and zap and zest day
A plenty to digest day
Friday is Chip Day

Friday is a cool day
A love to go to school day
An only just one rule day:
Friday is Chip Day

Friday is a fave day
A never misbehave day
An eat the food you crave day
Friday is Chip Day

Grab vinegar, salt and tomato sauce
When that day comes around of course
If you're hungry enough to eat a horse
Don't worry...
Because
Friday is Chip Day

Mum's got a Baby growing inside Her

Mum's got a baby growing inside her
Mum's getting larger, fatter and wider
It really is a massive lump
She calls it her big belly bump
Mum saw its picture on TV
In somewhere called Maternity

Tiny mouth
Tiny nose
Tiny feet
Tiny toes
Tiny arms
Tiny legs
Tiny body
Tiny head

Mum's got a baby in her tummy
Making her look round and funny
It's hiding underneath her top
Pretty soon I think she'll...POP!
Though it will make us very happy
I don't want to change its nappy

Tiny ears
Tiny eyes
Tiny knees
Tiny thighs
Tiny smile
Tiny gums
Tiny chest
Tiny bum

Mum's new baby under her blouse
Will soon be living in our house
Our family will then be four
And not a threesome anymore
We're all in an excited state
It's due next Friday - we can't wait

Tiny dummy
Tiny cot
Tiny wee-wee
Tiny pot
Tiny clothes
Tiny toys
Tiny girl
Or tiny boy?

Mum's got a baby growing inside her
Mum's getting larger, fatter and wider

There's Nothing like a GOAL!

See the home support exploding
As emotions are unloading
Thunderbolts or two-yard toe-ins
Will top all excitement polls
'Cause there's nothing like a
GOAL!

You'll forgive all of those misses
Rediscover what true bliss is
All around you hugs and kisses
Now your team is on a roll
'Cause there's nothing like a
GOAL!

Till that point the game was boring
With the commentator snoring
Now as one the crowd is roaring
Dig that sound in both ear holes
'Cause there's nothing like a
GOAL!

More dazzling than the brightest light
More thrilling than a fast motorbike
More pulsating than a rocket in flight
More satisfying than a gigantic bite
From the biggest, juiciest burger
Shout it so the whole world's heard ya?
'Cause there's nothing like a
GOAL!

It's a striker's greatest pleasure
It's what football fans most treasure
Watch the replay at your leisure
Then watch it again
And again
And again
And again
To lift your heart
Soothe your pain
And electrify your soul
'Cause there's nothing like a
GOAL!

Mr Onomatopoeia

I'm someone you'll want to know
Mr Onomatopoeia
Helping you spell every sound
That goes into your ears

Crocodiles I make them SNAP!
Windows I make SMASH!
Bees in springtime I make BUZZ!
Cars I make them CRASH!

I'm Mr Onomatopoeia
The SQUELCH in your wet welly
Though difficult enough to say
It's harder still to spell me

Ghosts and ghouls I make them WOOOOOH!
Balloons I make them POP!
Chattering children I make SHHHHH!
Rain I make DRIP, DROP! PLIP, PLOP!
DRIP, DROP! PLIP, PLOP!
DRIP, DROP! PLIP, PLOP!
Until the storm or shower stops

The loudest neighbour in your street
I cause bombs to BOOM!
Write your noises like you hear them
And you'll top your class real soon

I make angry lions ROAAAAR!
Big Ben I make him BONG!
Fingertips I make them CLICK!
Door bells I make DING-DONG!
DING-DONG!

I hope you're glad you met me
Mr Onomatopoeia
Helping you spell every sound
That goes into your ears

That goes into your ears
With onomatopoeia

Stop Fiddling!

Don't fiddle with your pencil
Don't fiddle with your pen
Don't fiddle with your paper
I won't tell you again
Don't fiddle with your hair
Don't fiddle with your chair
Don't tug your tie
Or your underwear
STOP FIDDLING!

Don't fiddle with your face
Or your pencil case
Don't fiddle with your socks
Or your shoelace
Focus, focus
Concentrate
Don't talk to yourself
Don't talk to your mates
STOP FIDDLING!

You're tapping
You're flicking
You're fidgeting
You're clicking
You're pushing
You're picking
You're rustling
You're kicking
And you're twiddling...
STOP FIDDLING!

Don't fiddle with your ruler
Your rubber or watch
Leave your lunchbox alone
It's only ten o'clock
Point those ears in my direction
Give me one hundred per cent attention
STOP FIDDLING!

Don't fiddle with your rucksack
Or your sports kit
Put down that football
Don't play with it
Be still
Stone-like
Be statuesque
Sit up straight
Be silent
Stop getting me stressed
Put your hands face down upon your desk
These are simple instructions to digest
So please - give it a rest and...
STOP FIDDLING!

Scared of the Dark

You can hear my knees are knocking
You can feel my heartbeat stopping
'Cause I'm scared, I'm so scared of the dark

My hands are hot and sweaty
While my legs wobble like jelly
'Cause I'm scared, I'm so scared of the dark

I'm an adult fully grown up
But don't leave me here alone Mum
'Cause I'm scared, I'm so scared of the dark

Pyjamas on I'm ready
To be cuddling my teddy
'Cause I'm scared, I'm so scared of the dark

Vicious vampires with eyes blood-red
Lurk with werewolves under my bed
'Cause I'm scared, I'm so scared of the dark

See that monster's shadow near me
All is spooky, creepy, eerie
'Cause I'm scared, I'm so scared of the dark

I hide behind my settee
So that yeti will not get me
'Cause I'm scared, I'm so scared of the dark

And that banging in the wardrobe
Makes me slide under my bedclothes
'Cause I'm scared, I'm so scared of the dark

Hold my hand and leave the light on
Late at night when I am frightened
'Cause I'm scared, I'm so scared of the dark

I jump out my socks and shoes too
When the ghosts and ghouls go
WOOOOOOOOH...WOOOOOOOOH!
'Cause I'm scared, I'm so scared of the dark

I'm scared, I'm so scared of the dark

Puddles

What can beat the special thrill of jumping into puddles?
It excites me
It delights me
Though it *does* land me in trouble

I like to get
Others wet
It's great fun bursting bubbles
But what can beat the special thrill of jumping into puddles?

Nothing tops me stamping hard upon the flooded ground
Then spraying pints of puddle muck everywhere around
Drenching people passing by when they least expect it
Not caring that their happy day is spoilt because I wrecked it

I love the splash
I love the splosh
I love the soggy sounds
Yes, nothing tops me stamping hard upon the flooded ground

Stomping in those pavement pools - it's simply the best
Though water flows through overclothes and to my pants and vest
Bouncing like a kangaroo
Till there's squelching in my shoe
I leap
I dive
I misbehave
I cause a mini tidal wave

Are you feeling sad or down
Gloomy or depressed?
Try stomping in those pavement pools - it's simply the best

Treading in those tiny lakes of rain is really cool
Though I'm 53 I'm not too old to act the fool

So I'll find the most gigantic puddle
That's what I plan to do
Now step aside
Run and hide
Or I'm gonna soak you
And you and you and you and you and you and you and you

I'm a Chocoholic

I'm a chocoholic 'cause I just can't get enough of it
I'm a chocoholic ever scoffing it and stuffing it
Milk chocolate, white chocolate, dark chocolate - I don't care
I'd sell my little sister for a single scrumptious square
What word whizzes through my thoughts again and again?
That wonderful word beginning with 'ch' - I've chocolate on
the brain

What do I like?
Chocolate
What do I bite?
Chocolate
All day and night?
Chocolate
Not Polos, chewing gum or Turkish delight
But Chocolate

I'm a chocoholic so I want to have a bath in it
I'm a chocoholic I'll float ten large chocolate tarts in it
I'm getting wider, heavier and fatter
But I'm a chocoholic so it doesn't really matter
Chocolate cereal
Chocolate eggs
I'm growing chunky chocolate arms and chewy chocolate legs
My dentist says "You have to stop!"
But I don't care if my teeth rot
So long as I can have a lot
Of chocolate

What's got me obsessed?
Chocolate
What gives my life zest?
Chocolate
What food is the best?
Chocolate
When I open my mouth what can you smell upon my breath?
Chocolate

I'm a chocoholic I'll kill for that cocoa flavouring
I'm a chocoholic it's my favourite snack for savouring
Chocolate yogurt
Chocolate spread
Hot chocolate when I go to bed
My mind is often finding that it's all that's in my head
Please – bury me inside a chocolate coffin when I'm dead

What food tastes sooooo neat?
Chocolate
What food do I eat?
Chocolate
What food can't you beat?
Chocolate
When you look inside my burger buns you'll not see any meat
But chocolate
C.h.o.c.o.l.a.t.e.
Guess what I'm having for my tea?
Chocolate

Pillar Box Pete

Pete was eaten by a pillar box
It grabbed him and gobbled him, spat out his socks
He ignored all the warnings or maybe forgot
The dangers of slipping his hand in that slot

Pete's parcel got munched up and crunched up for starters
While he was provided for dinner and afters
Resembling scenes from some horror movie
Poor Pete was converted from human to smoothie

His screams could be heard by shocked passers-by
As Pete became filling for envelope pie
The postman who opened the box was surprised
To find tonnes of slush and mush slopping inside

And how many more people vanish this way
Who go to post letters then aren't seen again?
So stop and consider (with Pete presumed dead)
When you next send a message - try email instead

My Pen

My pen is my pal
My pen is my chum
My pen can write any word under the sun
When we work together it's hours of fun

He touches the paper and ink starts to run
And roll
And flow
Never quite knowing where our poem will go
Them rhythms!
Them rhymes!
I'm tapping my toes...

My pen cost me five pounds
An absolute bargain
When resting he frequently doodles in margins
Or sits in my pocket
Or lies on my desk
Please take back your pencil
My pen is the best
(For a small fee he'll help you in your spelling test)

Blue plastic bottom
Shiny gold top
When we're inspired we're hot, hot, hot
Scribing and scribbling until we drop

My pen is pure power when held in my hand
He looks at the world and he understands
Making you laugh
Making you frown
Making you smile
Bringing you down
Making you happy
Making you cry
Making you sad
Lifting you high

He shares my emotions
My opinions
My voice
If my pen was a car
He'd be a Rolls Royce

Without him I'm silent
With a knot in my tongue
My pen is my pal
My pen is my chum

The Detention Rap

When school finished at half past three
I didn't go home unfortunately
'Cause I messed around in history
Chemistry, biology and literacy
My teacher said I had to pay the penalty

I got a detention
I got a detention
Sir said I attract too much negative attention
If I attract any more I'll receive a suspension
What did I get?
I got a detention

My punishment was writing many essays and lines
On how to show respect and listen all the time
Concentrate on sharpening those ears of mine
What was the sentence imposed for my crime?

I got a detention
I got a detention
My timetable had an hour extension
You walked home while I walked in the other direction
What did I get?
I got a detention

I acted like the class clown and then I got caught
I'm worried about what will be in my report
Though I pleaded like an innocent "It wasn't my fault"
Teacher said it's a lesson I must be taught

I got a detention
I got a detention
I was going to be a prefect now I'm out of contention
If you see my Mum it's something you shouldn't mention
What did I get?
I got a detention

So don't follow the bad example
I've set you
Or you'll end up
With a detention too
What will you get?
You'll get a detention

My moany Neighbour

I've got a moany neighbour
Who always is complaining
She doesn't like the weather hot
And whinges when it's raining

She hates it when it's quiet
But despises too much noise
She grumbles when I play outside
With other girls and boys

She says dogs are deplorable
And cannot cope with cats
She gives abuse to refuse trucks
She thinks they bring in rats

She shouts "YOUR TV'S MUCH TOO LOUD!"
While banging on our wall
She nags us in the holidays
But whines when we're at school

She's angry with the pensioner
At number thirty-eight
She carps about the squeaking sound
Of our old rusty gate

She criticises window cleaners
And the postmen too
Every night she remonstrates
Each time we flush our loo

No matter where Dad parks his car
She cries "THAT'S MY PARKING SPACE!"
If you saw her you'd know her
By her scary stony face
She moans about the driveways
She moans about road signs
She moans about the potholes
She moans about the crime
She moans about the gardens
She moans about the litter
She moans about the Council Tax
She's miserable and bitter
She moaned when we moved in
She's moaning 'cause we're going
She saw my website yesterday
Now she's moaning about this poem

Mr Elastic

I stretch to the Moon
I stretch to the stars
To Jupiter, Saturn
And way beyond Mars
I stretch my muscles to make myself stronger
In the whole wide world there's nobody longer
I stretch into the garden
Down the hall and up the stairs
I stretch under rugs, carpets
Tables and chairs
I've been like this since I was created
I live my life forever elongated

I'm a friendly, bendy, never-ending man
Mr Elastic that's who I am

I stretch down the bakers
To buy a loaf of bread
I'll need a fifty-foot grave
To bury me in when I'm dead
I love to see the shock on strangers' faces
When I *don't* kneel down to tie my shoelaces
I stretch up high
I stretch wide and low
I stretch my head
Shoulders, knees and toes
(I can even stretch my nose)
I stretch up the ladder to the window cleaner
And quickly contract like a cool concertina

I'm a friendly, bendy, never-ending man
Mr Elastic that's who I am

I stretch to Mount Everest
Skyscrapers and aeroplanes
Through manhole cover cracks
Along sewers and drains
From a sitting down position I mend broken lights
You'll not find a tape measure half my height
I stretch to the bottom
I reach the top
I stretch to Kings Cross Station
And my local bus stop
People say "Be careful or you might snap"
I say "Don't dismay, I'm OK, I'm a stretchable chap"

I'm a friendly, bendy, never-ending man
Mr Elastic that's who I am

My Teacher's got Eyes in the Back of Her Head

My teacher's got eyes in the back of her head
So you'd better listen to what she said
She probably knows what you're doing
Even when you're in bed
If you muck about
Don't you know she'll catch you out?
It's one false move and you're dead

You're never out of her sights
So watch out where you tread
Where's my teacher got eyes?
In the back of her head

My teacher's got ears in strange places too
If someone talks on assembly then she always knows who
She gave me detention because I spoke to you
If you say a word
Don't you know that you'll be heard?
But how she does it I haven't a clue

She's got x-ray vision
She'll fill you with dread
Where's my teacher got eyes?
In the back of her head

My teacher knows when I'm telling lies
I think she's employing an army of spies
I say "Dog ate my homework Miss" but she's too wise
When you tell any fib
Don't you know she'll know you did?
She'll say "Stop telling porky pies"

So don't mess with my teacher
Pick another instead
Where's my teacher got eyes?
In the back of her head

I'm a spare Spare Rib

I'm a spare spare rib lying cold in your fridge
I once was hot
Then someone forgot
To serve me up with the other lot
And as nobody returned me to the pot
I'm a spare spare rib

In barbecue sauce
I come from a pig not a cow or horse
You could have had me for starters or for your main course
But you didn't...
So I'm a spare spare rib

No.42
On the local Chinese takeaway menu
Abandoned at the back of the queue
Like a single sock or a solitary shoe
I'm a spare spare rib

A bit of meat sitting on some bone
Contemplating a future alone
In this silver foil dish I now call my home
I'm sorry to moan
And moan and moan
But I'm a spare spare rib

No longer looking so appealing
I'm chewy and tough and my gravy's congealing
So don't over-order when you get your next meal in
'Cause remember we ribs too have feelings
I'm a spare spare rib

It's so not fair
I could have tasted terrific cooked medium rare
But I was left by myself when everyone had their share
So I'm a spare rib going spare

Itch

I've got an itch I cannot scratch
Right in the middle of my back
It drives me nuts all day and night
A maddening mosquito bite

I want to shout I want to scream
I want to cover it in cream
I want to slice it with a saw
I want to roll around the floor
I want to stab it with a stick
I want to bash it with a brick

What makes me twist and turn and twitch?
My itch, itch, itch

I cannot see it with my eyes
It can't be reached although I try
I've never had an itch so bad
The worst itch that I've ever had

I want to jab it with a fork
I want to burn it with a torch
I want to poke it with a pen
And afterwards poke it again
I want to freeze it with some ice
I want to cut it with a knife

What makes me twist and turn and twitch?
My itch, itch, itch

I can't sit still I have to move
There's no cure for these itchy blues
Just like a feather down my shirt
I itch so much it almost hurts
I want to prick it with a pin
I want to bung it in a bin
I want to claw it with my nails
I want to banish it to Wales
I want to rub it with a rock
I want to slap it with a sock

What makes me twist and turn and twitch?
My itch, itch, itch

Who'd have thought a tiny tickle
Could get me in such a pickle?
My itch, itch itch

Worms

Worms are giving me creeps
Worms will get me in my sleep
Worms are sliding through the grass
Worms still squirm when cut in half
Worms have got no feet or hands
Worms make wormholes in the sand
Worms are all spaghetti-shaped
Worms go crispy when they're baked
Worms will drill my apple through
Worms can't jump like kangaroos
Worms are breeding in my shed
Worms - be careful where you tread!
Worms are all symmetrical
Worms are soft and bendable
Worms can wiggle, worms can twitch
Worms for dinner makes me sick
Worms are sneaking down my shirt
Worms are sliming up your skirt
Worms are quite despicable
Worms aren't very lickable
Worms are moving in the mud
Worms like lapping up my blood
Worms are thin, fat, short and long
Worms will eat me when I'm gone
Wooooooooooooooooooooooorms!

My Superpower

My mate Max has laser vision
Melting metal with perfect precision
Browning toast
And the Sunday roast
Who has his own show on television?
My mate Max who has laser vision

My cousin Kate can teleport
Changing location with a single thought
In the blink of an eye
England to Dubai
Who moves from country to country without a passport?
My cousin Kate who can teleport

My buddy Bill can shrink to ant-size
When he does you can never fail to be surprised
Though possessing human strength
At one millimetre in length
Who still has to be wary of hungry flies?
My buddy Bill who can shrink to ant-size

My pal Pete is telekinetic
He can move any object by looking at it
Shifting the fridge
Lifting a bridge
Who do all the girls call totally terrific?
My pal Pete who is telekinetic

My sister Sara can change her shape
Yesterday an octopus, today an ape
Often hard to recognise
The queen of disguise
Who morphs from a camel into a snake?
My sister Sara who can change her shape

But I can't turn invisible, run extra-fast or fly
As a poet I thought "I'm just an ordinary guy"
Then I saw I could inspire
I could engage
I could make people listen, read and turn over a page
Unlock creativity
Spark imagination
Master the skill of communication

So if YOU want a superpower too
Whether you're a girl or guy
Get typing
Get writing
And give poetry a try

Feet

Feet, feet, feet

Feet can be short or fat or long
Feet that aren't washed poo and pong

Feet help you go for a walk
Feet can't ever, ever talk

Feet stretch upwards to make us taller
Feet are 12 inches on old-fashioned rulers

Feet can be very hairy
Feet can be very scary

Feet have normally got five toes
Feet travel with you wherever you go

Feet paddle in water in the sun
Feet join the legs that let you run

Feet usually come in twos
Feet keep warm in socks and shoes

Feet stand firmly on the ground
Feet are there when you look down

Feet are found in fours on dogs and cats
Feet that are muddy are wiped on doormats

Feet love to move
Feet tap to music and dance and groove

Feet get us from A to B
Feet take steps – 1, 2, 3
Feet like to rest when the long day is done
Feet are freaky, fantastic, fabulous, and fun

Feet, feet, feet

Grandad drives a Tank

When Grandad picks me up from school
Everyone says "Wow, that's cool!"
On the road he breaks all rules
Grandad drives a tank

He fought in it in World War Two
It flies the flag - red, white and blue
Keep your TARDIS Doctor Who
Grandad drives a tank

He can ride it where he likes
Crushes cars and bashes bikes
Don't make him angry or uptight
Grandad drives a tank

I love to sit inside its cockpit
Give the turret a spin
Shout aloud "Up periscope!"
Bully me you'd never win
Surrounded by this metal skin
I'm a sardine in a mighty tin

At first it seemed quite strange to us
My teacher cried "It's dangerous"
I never catch a train or bus
Grandad drives a tank

Dig them caterpillar tracks
Dig that armour - front, side, back
Careful 'cause he could attack
Grandad drives a tank

He takes it out on shopping runs
Scares the high street with the guns
It's just his way of having fun
Grandad drives a tank

His vehicle choice is unusual
A massive mean machine
It's parked outside his house at night
Camouflaged in brown and green
Right next to his submarine
I can't wait till I'm seventeen
Then I'll drive Grandad's tank

He's a P.I.G

He never ever has enough
Although he's full he'll stuff and stuff
Three cakes, four buns and a Crunchie too
His belly bounces more than a kangaroo
He'll slurp and gobble, gulp and chew
Because he is a pig
He's a pig
He's a pig
He's a P.I.G
His diet's a catastrophe
If you met him then you'd agree
That he's a P.I.G

His appetite is never-ending
It's grub not people he's befriending
Ten meals a day is just a snack
He shops in Sainsbury's with a sack
He's gonna have a heart attack
Because he is a pig
He's a pig
He's a pig
He's a P.I.G
At dinner he's in ecstasy
You eat for one he eats for three
Yes he's a P.I.G

He swallowed up twelve loaves of bread
His doctor said "He should be dead"
His breakfast is a whole horse baked
His lunch is fifteen fillet steaks
He burps and starts a huge earthquake
Because he is a pig
He's a pig
He's a pig
He's a P.I.G
Butter, biscuits, pork pies, cheese
Check out his larder then you'll see
Why he's a P.I.G

He ate the dog's food and the cat's
Addicted to full-cream and fat
He even eats asleep at night
Some say his mouth should be sewn tight
Hold on to your head he might take a bite
Because he is a pig
He's a pig
He's a pig
He's a P.I.G
Devouring every calorie
He'll eat YOUR dinner too for tea
He's a greedy P.I.G

The Yuck Truck

The Yuck Truck
Collects all our muck
The rubbish
The dirt, dust and grime
On Monday mornings
I'm sleeping and snoring
But it wakes me up every time

Then the Yuck Truck
Snorts up and sucks up
The junk
And crams it all in
It rattles
It bashes
It grates, grinds and crashes
The boxes, the bags and the bins

It shakes
It shudders
While squeaking breaks judder
It wobbles
And bobbles along
It's stinky
It's smelly
It took our old telly
You'll know that it's here by its horrible pong

The Yuck Truck
Collects all the muck
'Cause that's what it was built to do
Wood, metal, plastic
Glass and elastic
Though some's now recycled to new

The Yuck Truck
It wheezes and whines
Swallows up refuse
The sludge and the slime
But still gets back to the depot by nine
Leaving my street looking shiny and clean
Fantastically fine
Plush and pristine
Till the same time next week
When it comes round again
Gobbling up the new garbage
That we've made by then

The Yuck Truck
Collects all our muck
The rubbish
The dirt, dust and grime
On Monday mornings
I'm sleeping and snoring
But it wakes me up every time

Custard Man

I'm Custard Man
Give me custard, man
On pudding, on pie, on fruit, on flan
Banana flavour, vanilla or chocolate
Serve me some I'll slurp the lot of it
Strawberry sauce or raspberry jam
Don't fit in with my master plan
All I desire is custard, man

I love it in a can or tin
I love it when it's runny thin
I love it so much it's a sin
I'd even drink it from your bin

I'm Custard Man
Give me custard, man
On pork, on peas, on lettuce, on lamb
If I found four bowls of blancmange
I'd soak them up just like a sponge
Once my meals were dull and bland
Now I'm this liquid's biggest fan
I want to live in Custardland

I love it whether cold or hot
I love it with the skin on top
I love it so much I can't stop
Until I taste the final drop

I'm Custard Man
Give me custard, man
On spaghetti, on stew, on haddock, on ham
I hate hot dogs smothered in mustard
My rule is it's cool to be caked in custard
None of my friends can understand
They say my craving's out of hand
But I reply "More custard, man!"

I love it when it's set and thick
I always love to have a lick
I love it till I'm feeling sick
This habit is too hard to kick

Why scream for ice cream
When it isn't my scene
And only one thing
Fulfils my dreams?
For starter, sweet and in-between
I'm a fellow liking yellow
Not red or blue or green
I'm Custard Man
I'm the Custard King
Give me custard, custard, custard!

Cool Addiction

My head is stuck inside this book
I only meant to take a look
Till I saw what had been written
Instantly my mind was smitten
In a land of fascination
Sparking my imagination
Passions burning like a flame
Pictures dancing in my brain

My head is stuck inside this book
Just one page was all it took
I was focused and engaged
Thrilled, enthralled and entertained
Title, cover - so inviting
Words speak to me - so exciting
Such adventure, such intrigue
In a world of make believe

My head is stuck inside this book
Superglued, completely hooked
Unaware of all around me
Once this magic story found me
Characters feel like my friends
Plot unfolding till the end
Whether fact or whether fiction
Reading is a cool addiction

I live in a Bin

I live in a bin
I live in a bin
Feel free to lift the lid, drop rubbish in

I don't care if it reeks
I don't care if it whiffs
I don't care if it pongs
I don't care if it niffs

People say I make them queasy
'Cause my body odour's cheesy
My skin is rank, my hair is greasy

I live in a bin
A garbage bin
With sacks of stinky socks, potato skins
Broken glass, metal, plastic
Junk is cool
Junk's fantastic
Pour mustard pickle on my head
Along with bits of mouldy bread
Why should I buy a house instead?

I live in a bin
It's where I reside
Though air is clearer on the other side
I savour the sweet stench of pollution
Got a waste problem?
I'm the solution
Does my existence cause you confusion?

I live in a bin
By your garden gate
Flies and maggots treat me as their mate
I cohabit with a couple of rats
We wine and dine, we chat and chat
While chewing rind and bones and fat
From the meal you had last night
Washed down with sour Angel Delight
And a half-empty bottle of gin

I live in a bin
Too cold in snow
Too hot in sun
Nevertheless it's fun, fun, fun
Collecting trash by the tonne
I lollop in oil and swim in scum
Why do you think I'm always smelling?
It's 'cause of this bin I have for a dwelling
If you sniffed me it's a sure way of telling
I live in a bin!

There's a SSSSSSnake in My Shoe

There's a SSSSSSnake in my shoe
Escaped from the zoo
He's enormous
Maybe poisonous
So dangerous too

There's a SSSSSSnake in my shoe
Stretched out in full view
He's kind of long
And big and strong
And orange, red and blue

There's a SSSSSSnake in my shoe
He's snoring fast asleep
I've nudged him
But can't budge him
He's just lying in a heap

There's a SSSSSSnake in my shoe
Now curled up in a ball
I've asked my Mum
If he can come
Along with me to school

There's a SSSSSSnake in my shoe
He says his name is Keith
And that he'll stay
At least three days
While showing me his teeth

There's a SSSSSSnake in my shoe
A rattle SSSSSSnake I think
I've fed him cake
Some fillet steak
And bowls of milk to drink

There's a SSSSSSnake in my shoe
You can hear him hiSSSSSSing
He has no feet
Though seems quite sweet
I won't suggest you kiss him

There's a SSSSSSnake in my shoe
He eats children up - it's true!
So I won't annoy him
Just enjoy him
I guess that's the best thing to do
Don't you?

There's a SSSSSSnake in my shoe

67

Magnetic Me

Magnetic Me
Magnetic Me

Anything and everything sticks to me
Carpets, cars, books, TVs
Pencils, pens and bumblebees
Tables, trousers, front door keys
Newspapers and DVDs

Magnetic Me
Magnetic Me

It happens totally naturally
I've an instant connectivity
Defying the laws of gravity
Come near you'll adhere instantly

Magnetic Me
Magnetic Me

Scientists they all agree
I've a very unusual biology
I'm the gluiest person in history
I'm a gent like cement you can't shake free

Magnetic Me
Magnetic Me

More power than a magnet factory
Shake hands you'll be stuck by the count of three
One look you'll be hooked like a fish in the sea
I've a magnetic personality

Magnetic Me
Magnetic Me

I'm an
M.A.G.
N.E.T.
What's my name?
Magnetic Me!

Russell the Brussels Sprout

I'm Russell the Brussels Sprout
A roughy
A toughy
A beast
And a lout
I bully my way onto your plate
I'm rude
I'm crude
I'm the food you most hate
Bad Bill Broccoli is my best mate
I'm Russell the Brussels Sprout

I'm small
So uncool
A poisonous ball
Awfully obnoxious
And not sweet at all
Can you think of a more horrid vegetable
Than me - Russell the Brussels Sprout?

I'll ruin your delicious Christmas dinner
Give you frightening nightmares as well
If you want `disgusting' then I'm a winner
I'm cooked in the kitchens of hell

I'm mean
I'm green
Utterly obscene
You'd prefer a cute carrot or a beautiful bean
Cover me in ketchup
Smother me in sauce
Drown me in gravy
I'll still spoil your main course
If I'm finally swallowed it's often by force
I'm Russell the Brussels Sprout

I'm deadly and foul
I'm putrid and rotten
And bitter – so best left in Tesco forgotten
I'm the storm cloud to spoil the sunniest day
'Cause I make so much wind that I'll blow you away
All children scream "YUCK!" when they see me and say
"I don't want Russell the Brussels Sprout"

My Computer died last Night

My computer died last night
After many repairs he gave up his fight
With one last hug
I pulled out his plug
And out went his monitor light

He was part of the family
A very special relation
Storing my folders, documents, photos
And personal information
I used words like 'great loss', 'gutted' and 'devastation'
As my IT
Was consigned to history
When my computer died last night

He knew so much about me
With each keystroke we grew closer
Displaying so much more intelligence
Than the my vacuum cleaner, TV or toaster

I'll miss his silver casing
His keyboard and his mouse
I'll miss his warm and welcoming screen
When returning home to my house
I'll miss his Bart Simpson wallpaper
His processor's gentle hum
Surfing the Net together we had tonnes and tonnes of fun
Of all the computers in the whole wide PC world
He was my special one

I'll still reminisce about the files we shared
Upgrading his memory
Installing the latest software
From megabytes to kilobytes to gigabytes to deep despair
When my computer died last night

His metal body's now with the waste
But his spirit wanders in cyberspace
With his mind preserved and alive
On a portable hard drive
Waiting someday to be reconnected
To a new machine...and then resurrected

So despite holding a funeral
I had no need to be sad at all
When my computer died last night

The Day My Underwear went BOOM!

The day my underwear went BOOM!
Exploding like a burst balloon
The noise was heard upon the moon
The day my underwear went...

...POP!
Windows wobbled, ceilings rocked
It was expensive, from Top Shop
But still my underwear went...

...BANG!
Along my street the echoes rang
What happened? No-one could explain
The day my underwear went...

...ZAP!
The cat leapt six foot off my lap
I got inspired to write this rap
The day my underwear went...

...BUST!
Vests vaporised, pants turned to dust
I heaved a sigh of deep disgust
The day my underwear went...

...BAM!
I was an underwearless man
With one burnt thread left in my hand
The day my underwear went...

... BOOM!
A choking smoke consumed my room
My normal life can't be resumed
Because my underwear went...

...BOOM!

HOMEWORK!

My teacher makes it clear to me
That if I want to top the tree
In English, Maths, Geography
Biology and History
Then get to university
My timetable won't end at three
But I must beg to disagree
Don't want to do my
HOMEWORK!

Back in my house returned from school
My brain is strained and feeling full
What I face next is harsh and cruel
There's no respite or rest at all
I want to chill out and be cool
Go ride my bike or kick a ball
Why can't I flout one tiny rule?
Don't want to do my
HOMEWORK!

Revision then a practice test
Jam cramming facts I can't digest
I'm losing all my zap and zest
Though Miss tells me that she knows best
I'm well and truly unimpressed
It's like I'm climbing Everest
Why risk a cardiac arrest?
Don't want to do my
HOMEWORK!

I do it when I watch TV
I do it when I eat my tea
I do it surreptitiously
At night in bed when none can see
All work, no play's a recipe
For guaranteeing misery
A ball and chain is tied to me
Don't want to do my
HOMEWORK!

Already I've a bad headache
More studying's too much to take
Forever keeping me awake
This camel's back is bound to break
I'll crumble like a Cadbury Flake
Wish I could stage the great escape
Sir set me free for goodness sake
Don't want to do my
HOMEWORK!

So Slow Sloth

I'm So Slow Sloth hanging upside down
In pain I strain to get around
Living life at my own pace
I'm always last in any race

I hardly ever move an inch
You rarely see my muscles flinch
I crawl along from A to B
Some time next week I might reach C

I'm unexcited, uninspired
My batteries have been de-wired
Doing nothing is my aim
Boredom occupies my brain

I'm static, still and statuesque
I have to go now - time to rest
I'm So Slow Sloth that's what I said
Yawning my way back to bed
Yes I'm So Slow Szzzzzzzzzzzzzzzzzzzzzzz

ARACHNOPHOBIA!

There's a spider crawling up my leg
A spider sleeping in my bed
A spider living in my shed
One in my chicken sandwich sucking on my slice of bread

I want to scream
I want to shout
I want to tear my hair out
I want to shriek
I'm feeling sick
Please someone dial 999 quick
My friends say "Neal – what's wrong with ya?"
I say "ARACHNOPHOBIA!"

There's a spider wedged between my toes
A cobweb hanging from my nose
A spider chewing on my clothes
A spider moving in to make my wardrobe his new home

I'm panting
I'm sweating hot
I'm frozen stiff, stuck to this spot
I'm horrified
I'm petrified
My stomach's churning up inside
My friends say "Neal – what's wrong with ya?"
I say "ARACHNOPHOBIA!"

A spider's sitting in my chair
Another's tangled in my hair
There's a spider here, a spider there
Three spiders in my underwear
I want to yell
I want to flee
There's a spider swimming in my tea
I want to faint
I want to vomit
I can't even face reading Spider-Man comics
My friends say "Neal – what's wrong with ya?"
I say "ARACHNOPHOBIA!"

Some people are scared of the dark, snakes, flying or their teachers
Me? I'm absolutely terrified by them small eight-legged creatures
My friends say "Neal – what's wrong with ya?"
I say "ARACHNOPHOBIA!"

The Worry Box

I can't do long division
My head's a strange shape
I'm developing hairy toes
A big bully hit me
Gemma Jones bit me
There's a huge blue spot on my nose

I'm frightened of flies
Tom poked fun at my ears
I'm allergic to cranberry sauce
I'll never be rich
My sister's a witch
Jack said that I laugh like a horse

Je find French très confusing
I might need to wear glasses
Sam's driving me round the bend
I've spent all my savings
How long till I'm shaving?
Last week I was dumped by *two* girlfriends

Luke (who sits next to me)
Smells like rotting fish
I'm totally hopeless at sport
I'm scared of my Headteacher
I can't pronounce omonatopoeia...onomapatoemia...
onomatopoeia
Dad tore up my terrible school report

I think I've got nits
I'm dreading the dentist
My brain cannot work very fast
I can't spell Saskatchewan
My best mate's an alien
I'm so nervous of putting my hand up in class

Two back teeth are wobbly
I'm rubbish at poetry...
Whatever your stresses and fears
Just tell the Worry Box
Write to the Worry Box
And your problems will all disappear

My Sister's turned into a VAMPIRE

On the stroke of midnight
CLICK! Off went the light
I felt a nibble then a bite
My sister looked quite pale and white
And when she opened her mouth I got a massive fright
My sister's turned into a VAMPIRE

I heard blood dripping then an ear-splitting scream
She looked scarier than anyone that I'd ever seen
It was real – not a nightmare or the darkest of dreams
My sister's turned into a VAMPIRE

Her teeth grew sharp and long
She became powerful and strong
As ghastly as Godzilla
And a killer like King Kong
Where has my sweet little sister gone?
My sister's turned into a VAMPIRE

When she comes home from school I run and hide
I keep a mirror, cross and garlic forever by my side
The doctor said
"She's undead
"She's transmogrified"
My sister's turned into a VAMPIRE

She's moved to Transylvania
(That's a part of Romania)
Caught up in vampiremania
This poem could not get zanier
My sister's turned into a VAMPIRE

She likes to sleep in a coffin rather than her own bed
Her favourite colour is most definitely red
She swapped our cat for a bat that's made its home in our shed
It's doing in my head
My sister's turned into a VAMPIRE

So don't let her sink her fangs in you
It's not a healthy thing to do
She's now best friends with Dracula and Frankenstein too
It's true!
My sister's turned into a VAMPIRE

Yes if you see my sis
Don't let her give you a kiss
My sister's turned into a VAMPIRE

Never eat a whole Elephant Sandwich

Never eat a whole elephant sandwich
It's a daft thing to contemplate
You'd need three tonne of butter
You'd look a right nutter
And you'd end up cracking your plate

It's too big to fit in your lunch box
It's too big to fit in a case
It's too big to fit in your locker
It's too big to stuff in your face

Never eat a whole elephant sandwich
Your stomach would bang like a bomb
Proceed with great caution
Try small bite-sized portions
So you've room for some sweet later on

It's too big to put in your handbag
It's too big for your rucksack
It's too big to put in your fridge
It's too big to have as a snack

Never eat a whole elephant sandwich
Well that's what the zookeeper said
It will certainly fill you
Probably kill you
And besides
You'd run out of bread

Pop!

Bubble gum was great to chew
I'd blow it up and burst it too
Then chuck it high into the air
And watch it land...
In people's hair

More Poems to Enjoy by Neal Zetter

If **Bees in My Bananas** made you buzz with fun then Neal's
follow-up book of comedy poems, **It's Not Fine to Sit on a Porcupine**,
will make you tingle with excitement! It's another crazy rhyming
romp through topics as weird as a bored superhero, an angry shopping
trolley, a mammoth on the underground and even the world's worst
toilet! For ages 6-12 years but frequently enjoyed by those younger
and older and a classroom essential for teachers too.

One of Book Trust's 20 favourite children's poetry books.

*'An amusingly illustrated collection of humorous poems from an award-winning performance
poet, which covers a wide range of funny and interesting subjects'* BOOK TRUST

*'Rappy, happy poetic magic ... perfect for entertaining school classes or to be enjoyed by
all the family at home'* PAM NORFOLK, LANCASHIRE EVENING POST

Neal Zetter is a London-based comedy performance poet, author
and entertainer who uses poetry writing and performance to
develop literacy, confidence, self-expression, creativity
and presentation skills in 3 to 103 year olds.

See cccpworkshops.co.uk for more.

My First Performance Poetry books

SSSSNAP! 'Mister Shark, don't eat me up!'

An irresistible first performance poetry book encouraging readers to yell and clap their hands to SSSSTOP Mister Shark every time he tries to have a nibble.

Impossible not to join in with this SSSSUPER interactive poem's simple actions.

'Odd socks are all I ever wear, I cannot make a matching pair.'

Sounds familiar? In this first performance poetry book readers and listeners will enjoy calling out rhyming words and performing simple actions to create a lively, interactive poem.

Eye-catchingly colourful illustrations make these two books a perfect introduction to rhythm and rhyme.